How to Discover Your Purpose
in 10 Days
Prayers and Daily Journal

IS PRESENTED TO

_____

BY

_____

_____

_____

ON

_____

How to Discover Your

Purpose

in 10 Days

Prayers *and* Daily Journal

How to Discover Your

PURPOSE

in 10 Days

Prayers *and* Daily

Journal

Dr. J. Victor and
Catherine B. Eagan

WORKPLACE
WISDOM

SOUTHFIELD, MICHIGAN 48076 USA

Workplace Wisdom Publishing, LLC.,
17600 W. 12 Mile Road, Suite 1, Southfield, Michigan 48076.
www.workplacewisdompublishing.com • www.eaganbooks.com • 1-877-EAGANS1 (324-2671)

Publisher's Cataloging-in-Publication Data
(Prepared by The Donohue Group, Inc.)

Eagan, J. Victor.
    How to discover your purpose : prayers and daily journal / J. Victor
and Catherine B. Eagan.
        p. ; cm.
        ISBN: 1-932477-01-2
1. Diaries--Authorship. 2. Spiritual life. I. Eagan, Catherine B.
II. Title.

BF637.S4 E143 2004
808   2004110721

Cover Design by Brand Navigation — Bill Chiaravalle, Terra Petersen. www.brandnavigation.com
Interior Design by Pneuma Books, LLC. www.pneumabooks.com

Printed in the United States of America.
09 08 07 06 05   10 9 8 7 6 5 4 3 2 1

Acknowledgments

WE WOULD LIKE TO THANK:
Our Heavenly Father, for anointing and calling us to our purpose
Each other, for always supporting, loving, and encouraging one another
Our parents, whose love, prayers, and guidance inspired us
Our spiritual parents, Bishop Keith A. Butler and Minister Deborah Butler
And other gifted people whose dedication helped us write this book:
Bill Gothard, Institute in Basic Life Principles
Marilyn Hickey, Marilyn Hickey Ministries
Don and Katie Fortune, Authors
Dr. Myles Munroe, Chairman,
International Third World Leaders Association
Starra Pollard, our Executive Assistant
Lauren Doyle-Davis, our Personal Assistant
Pneuma Books, LLC, our Interior Designers
Brand Navigation, LLC, our Graphic Artists

Table of Contents

Introduction xi

Day 1: Discovering the Greatness Within. 1

Day 2: The Pathway to Discover Your Purpose —
The Formative Years. 15

Day 3: Narrowing Your Focus — Young Adulthood 29

Day 4: Obstacles on the Pathway to Purpose 41

Day 5: God's Unique Motivational Gifts —
Introduction/Perceiver. 55

Day 6: God's Unique Motivational Gifts — Server/Teacher. 71

Day 7: God's Unique Motivational Gifts — Exhorter/Giver 91

Day 8: God's Unique Motivational Gifts —
Administrator/Compassion. 111

Day 9: Maturing in Your Purpose — The Adult Years 131

Day 10: Fulfilling the Greatness Within 143

PURPOSE

INTRODUCTION

Introduction

Welcome to *How to Discover Your Purpose in 10 Days: God's Path to a Full and Satisfied Life.* This is a special edition of the purpose seminar that my wife and I have been teaching throughout the nation for the past decade. We are honored that God has given us the privilege of sharing fundamental principles for finding and fulfilling your purpose, and we are excited that you will be joining us on a 10-day journey to discovering God's plan for your life.

This system works. Read the teaching and complete the Action Plans and Self-Assessments that accompany each lesson. Use the *Prayers and Daily Journal* to write down your thoughts each day. We promise that if you diligently and prayerfully complete the 10-day process, God will begin to reveal to you His plans, desires, and purpose for your life.

There is nothing worse than wandering aimlessly in life, never reaching your full potential. God's best is for you to have success. This is possible when you walk in the fullness of what He has for you. God designed you to do great and mighty exploits on earth; and we pray that as you complete these 10-days you will begin to walk in the greatness that He preordained for you before the foundation of the world.

The material is life changing and it will be the same for you as it has been for countless others throughout the years. We are extremely excited for you! Our prayer is that God will reveal His specific purpose for your life and you will excel to the glory of God.

HOW TO USE THIS BOOK

How to Discover Your Purpose in 10 Days is designed to help you facilitate and identify your purpose. We as Christians are often told that God has a purpose for our lives; yet for many it is difficult to determine what that is. There are three types of people: those who do not know their God-given purpose; those who know their purpose, but are underdeveloped in it; and those who know their purpose, are developing it, and maturing.

No matter what stage of life you may be in right now, this book is for you!

How to Discover Your Purpose in 10 Days is a step-by-step, simple, yet comprehensive way to identify who God made you to be. It is an exciting journey to once and for all discover the greatness within you that God had in mind when He formed you in your mother's womb.

> Before I formed you in the womb I knew you; before you were
> born I sanctified you; I ordained you a prophet to the nations.
> JEREMIAH 1:5 (NKJV)

How to Discover Your Purpose in 10 Days is designed to propel you to new heights and teach you how to fulfill the perfect will of God for your life.

THE GOAL OF THE BOOK

The goal of *How to Discover Your Purpose in 10 Days* is to be a conduit in helping you understand your God-given, unique life assignment and unlock your personal greatness. At the same time, the book will help you feel good about yourself by helping you to understand yourself and others, including your family, your co-workers, children, boss, and friends.

The book is designed incrementally; and each day builds upon the other. To obtain the maximum results from the program it is strongly recommended that you undertake it day by day, prayerfully. With great excitement and anticipation we pray that after the 10 days have been completed, you will discover your purpose and begin to walk in God's best for your life.

THE STRUCTURE

How to Discover Your Purpose in 10 Days is designed so that each day takes you further along the pathway to discovering your God-given life purpose. As you prayerfully read and complete the associated exercises, you will begin to tap into the greatness within you.

Day 1: Discovering the Greatness Within

Day 1 marks the beginning of the exciting 10-day journey to your pathway to purpose. Day 1 reveals many of the awesome reasons why it is vitally important to identify and realize your God-given destiny.

Day 2: The Pathway to Discover Your Purpose — The Formative Years

In Day 2, you will discover how your purpose is intricately and progressively revealed to you by God. Even as a young child, your interests, natural talents, and abilities reflect the greatness God placed on the inside of you before birth. You were elaborately and intricately fashioned in the image of God Almighty and He formed you with a magnificent destiny in mind.

Day 3: Narrowing Your Focus — Young Adulthood

Day 3 focuses on the importance of determining your ruling passion and allowing it to govern your decisions on educational training, activities, and jobs that you undertake during young adulthood. God placed a ruling passion in you that reflects your innermost being. Uncovering your ruling passion is pivotal in discovering your God-given purpose.

Day 4: Obstacles on the Pathway to Purpose

Day 4 is the day of breakthrough! It reveals many of the obstacles that may arise along your pathway to purpose. There are countless reasons why you may get diverted, distracted, or thwarted from your pathway to purpose. Day 4 helps you locate yourself, make the necessary adjustments, and begin operating in your purpose.

Day 5: God's Unique Motivational Gifts — Introduction/Perceiver

In Day 5, the motivational gifts are introduced and the motivational gift of the Perceiver is discussed. God has called the Perceiver to intercede on the behalf of others and distinguish between right and wrong.

Day 6: God's Unique Motivational Gifts — Server/Teacher

In Day 6, the motivational gifts of Server and Teacher are revealed.

God has called the Server to perform the practical needs of others, while the Teacher has been anointed by God to manage and disseminate information.

Day 7: God's Unique Motivational Gifts — Exhorter/Giver

In Day 7, the motivational gifts of Exhorter and Giver are uncovered. God has called the Exhorter to encourage and build people up, while the Giver has been anointed by God to mobilize resources for the aid and benefit of others.

Day 8: God's Unique Motivational Gifts — Administrator/Compassion

In Day 8, the motivational gifts of Administrator and Compassion are outlined. God has called the Administrator to facilitate, administrate, and organize, while the Compassion gift is anointed by God to attend to and care for the emotional needs of others. Day 8 also answers the questions and challenges often faced in attempting to narrow down your motivational gift.

Day 9: Maturing in Your Purpose — The Adult Years

By Day 9, you should have begun to discover your God-given purpose. With this exciting revelation, you will learn how important it is to become more developed and mature in your purpose. It is God's desire that you dominate to His glory in your vocation. To do this, you must mature in your life work. Not only will you please God, you will also live a satisfied and fulfilled life.

Day 10: Fulfilling the Greatness Within

There is a great life work that the Lord is counting on you to fulfill. There is also an awesome destiny that God has prepared before the foundation of the world for you to realize. So, this power-packed series concludes on Day 10 centering on how to make your purpose a reality in your life.

You were fearfully and wonderfully made by God and He placed greatness on the inside of you before you were born. You have been called of God to do great and mighty exploits on earth and Day 10 reveals steps that will empower and enable you to soar in your life purpose.

Invite God to Help You

We suggest that prior to beginning each day of purpose that you pray and invite God to help you get revelation, knowledge, and understanding concerning the important information you are about to receive.

> Wisdom is the principal thing; Therefore get wisdom. And in all your getting, get understanding.
>
> PROVERBS 4:7 (NKJV)

We pray,

> That the God of our Lord Jesus Christ, the Father of glory, may give to you the spirit of wisdom and revelation in the knowledge of Him, the eyes of your understanding being enlightened; that you may know what is the hope of His calling, what are the riches of the glory of His inheritance in the saints, and what is the exceeding greatness of His power toward us who believe, according to the working of His mighty power.
>
> EPHESIANS 1:17-19 (NKJV)

Next, prepare your heart and mind in Christ Jesus. Earnestly seek understanding about how He created you and the unique purpose He planned for you to fulfill on earth — your special assignment, your life purpose.

But without faith it is impossible to please Him, for he who comes to God must believe that He is, and that He is a rewarder of those who diligently seek Him.

HEBREWS 11:6 (NKJV)

 When you see this icon, turn to *How to Discover Your Purpose in 10 Days* as instructed for additional information.

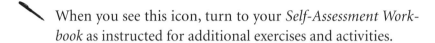 When you see this icon, turn to your *Self-Assessment Workbook* as instructed for additional exercises and activities.

Then, read each day's material, listen to the teaching, and complete the action plans and self-assessments that correspond to each day. They are designed to help you focus, identify areas for change, and receive the maximum benefit from the book.

Journal each day in your *Prayers and Daily Journal* and be careful not to overlook the small bits of information. Remember, we are carefully working on a puzzle that God has masterfully designed — you. So don't let any of the pieces get lost.

Purpose each day to embrace who God made you to be. Don't begrudge your uniqueness or belittle your importance. You are a royal priesthood and your contribution is important to the establishment of God's kingdom on earth. Know that He is depending on you to fulfill your purpose.

But you are a chosen generation, a royal priesthood, a holy nation, His own special people, that you may proclaim the praises of Him who called you out of darkness into His marvelous light.   1 PETER 2:9 (NKJV)

What is required of you is time, discipline, and commitment.

Lastly, be mindful that 10 days is a short period of time to resolve two of life's most fundamental and perplexing questions — Who am I? And what on earth am I here for? Our goal is to get you on the path to discovering your purpose. It can be the beginning of one of the best journeys of your Christian life.

Remember, *God* is expecting greatness from your life.

May the Lord richly bless you as you discover your purpose.

The Eagans

WORKPLACE
WISDOM

How to Discover Your

PURPOSE

in 10 Days

Prayers *and* Daily Journal

It is impossible to do everything people want you to do. You have just enough time to do God's will. Purpose-driven living leads to a simpler lifestyle and saner schedule.

RICK WARREN

A difficult time can be more readily endured if we retain the conviction that our existence holds a purpose — a cause to pursue, a person to love, a goal to achieve.

JOHN MAXWELL

Outstanding people have one thing in common: an absolute sense of mission.

ZIG ZIGLAR

The masterpiece of man is to live to the purpose.

BENJAMIN FRANKLIN

Multitudes of people, drifting aimlessly to and fro without a set purpose, deny themselves such fulfillment of their capacities, and the satisfying happiness which attends it. They are not wicked, they are only shallow. They are not mean or vicious; they simply are empty — shake them and they would rattle like gourds. They lack range, depth, and conviction. Without purpose their lives ultimately wander into the morass of dissatisfaction. As we harness our abilities to a steady purpose and undertake the long pull toward its accomplishment, rich compensations reward us. A sense of purpose simplifies life and therefore concentrates our abilities; and concentration adds power.

KENNETH HILDEBRAND

Singleness of purpose is one of the chief essentials for success in life, no matter what may be one's aim.

JOHN D. ROCKEFELLER

There is one quality which one must possess to win, and that is definiteness of purpose, the knowledge of what one wants, and a burning desire to possess it.

NAPOLEON HILL

PURPOSE

D A Y   O N E

Day 1 marks the beginning of the exciting 10-day journey on your pathway to purpose. Day 1 reveals many of the awesome reasons why it is vitally important to identify and realize your God-given destiny. You will also learn about the hidden problems of never discovering and fulfilling your life purpose.

1

Discovering the Greatness Within

- God has uniquely equipped each of us with innate abilities, gifts, and interests to enable us to fulfill our life purpose.

- You will never be completely satisfied or fulfilled until you are walking in God's plan for your life.

- God personally handcrafted you and placed certain gifts and abilities within you to fulfill a specific purpose in this life.

- Everything was created with a purpose and YOU are no exception.

- It is vitally important to your sense of worth and well-being to know and walk in God's perfect will for your life.

- Other people, including your spouse, children, family, co-workers, and friends will benefit from the awesome things God can do through you when you are operating in His divine plan for your life.

- No matter what decisions you have made in the past or how long it may take you to get into your purpose, the Lord will redeem the time you have lost when you make a decision to operate in and fulfill your God-given destiny.

- The highest level of anointing and blessing is available to you when you are in God's perfect will for your life.

- It pleases God when you walk in the purpose for which He created you.

 See Day One: Discovering the Greatness Within in *How to Discover Your Purpose in 10 Days.*

PRAYERFUL REFLECTION
Dear Heavenly Father, I thank You Lord and give You all the praise and glory. I pray that I will receive a revelation about what my purpose is; and I pray that as I write down my goals and complete the action plans and self-assessments on my 10-day journey to

---

Mark 9:23
*All things are possible to him
who believes.*

---

discovering my purpose, that You will birth in me who I am and who You created me to be.

Lord, forgive me, as I also I forgive myself, for the mistakes that I have made in the past and I open up my heart to receive all that You have in store for me.

It is no accident that I am here; You fashioned me in Your very own image with a specific and great destiny. I have a purpose and You have uniquely equipped me with special abilities and gifts to fulfill an important and mighty purpose on earth.

Lord, I know that you are a progressive God and I pray that as I read this book each day that you will begin to reveal the things that You have placed on the inside of me. I pray that You will start slowly and reveal my purpose to me day by day, now and for the rest of my life that I may fulfill the calling You have placed upon me. Thank You gracious Father for making my life purpose known to me. In Jesus' name, I pray. Amen.

DAY 1: ACTION PLAN

Please use the *Self-Assessment Workbook* as needed to complete the following items in your action plan.

1. Pray and thank God for creating you with a specific purpose.
2. Pray and ask God to reveal your specific purpose to you.
3. Whether you feel you are young or older, write down your life dreams here in your journal. (Ask God to reveal the dreams He placed inside of you.)

Colossians 3:23
And whatever you do,
do it heartily, as to the Lord, and not to men.

4. List 100 of your life goals here in your journal. Some examples include:
    - Receive a bachelor's degree in accounting
    - Own my own home decorating business
    - Purchase a four bedroom, two bath, ranch-style home
    - Secure investment properties, including apartment complexes and condominiums
    - Write a 200-page autobiography, chronicling my life
    - Travel to each continent
    - Amass $1 million in net worth
    - Have two children and raise them in the nurture and admonition of the Lord
    - Donate over $500,000 to my local church
    - Meet and marry the woman of my dreams and love her as Christ loves the church

5. Think about this question: If all of your financial needs were met in abundance, what would you enjoy doing everyday, for the rest of your life without getting paid for it and be happy?
6. Scripture meditation: Psalm 139:1-17, Psalm 8:1-9

DAY 1: JOURNAL

_____

_____

_____

Jeremiah 29:11
For I know the thoughts that I think toward you, says the LORD;
thoughts of peace and not of evil, to give you a future and a hope.

_____

_____

_____

_____

_____

_____

_____

_____

_____

_____

_____

_____

_____

_____

_____

Psalm 35:27 (NLT)
But give great joy to those who have stood with me in my defense.
Let them continually say, "Great is the LORD, who enjoys helping his servant."

Job 36:11
*If they obey and serve Him, They shall spend their days
in prosperity, And their years in pleasures.*

DAY ONE : PAGE 6

Psalm 37:23
The steps of a good man are ordered by the LORD,
And He delights in his way.

DAY ONE : PAGE 7

Jeremiah 33:3
Call to Me, and I will answer you,
and show you great and mighty things, which you do not know.

DAY ONE : PAGE 8

_____

_____

_____

_____

_____

_____

_____

_____

_____

_____

_____

_____

_____

_____

_____

_____

Philippians 4:13
I can do all things through Christ
who strengthens me.

_____

_____

_____

_____

_____

_____

_____

_____

_____

_____

_____

_____

_____

_____

Matthew 21:22
And whatever things you ask in prayer,
believing, you will receive.

_____

_____

_____

_____

_____

_____

_____

_____

_____

_____

_____

_____

_____

_____

Proverbs 16:3 (NLT)
*Commit your work to the LORD, and then
your plans will succeed.*

DAY ONE : PAGE 11

Psalm 16:11
You will show me the path of life; In Your presence is fullness of joy;
At Your right hand are pleasures forevermore.

DAY ONE : PAGE 12

PURPOSE

DAY TWO

In Day 2, you will discover how your purpose is intricately and progressively revealed to you by God. Even as a young child, your interests, natural talents, and abilities reflected the greatness God placed on the inside of you before birth. You were elaborately and intricately fashioned in the image of God Almighty and with a magnificent destiny in mind.

2

The Pathway to Discover Your Purpose – The Formative Years

- Your purpose is revealed incrementally.

- Purpose is the essence of our existence, so it is critical that you identify it.

- When you are in the early stages of growth before external influences either aid or hinder the expression of your motivational gift, natural behaviors reflect your God-given gifting.

- Parents are called by God to observe and identify their child's motivational gift.

- God has charged parents with the responsibility of placing their children in educational, religious, social, and extracurricular activities that support the maturation and development of their God-given abilities.

 See Day Two: The Pathway to Discover Your Purpose — The Formative Years in *How to Discover Your Purpose in 10 Days.*

PRAYERFUL REFLECTION FOR PARENTS
Lord, You have given me a powerful responsibility to identify and nurture the development and growth of my child(ren)'s God-given abilities. Lord, I accept this responsibility, and, according to James 1:5, I ask for wisdom in making decisions on behalf of my child(ren). May I only select those schools and activities that will support their God-given talents and abilities that they may grow and develop as You would have them. I thank You, Lord, for giving me insight to assist my child(ren) in growing and maturing in the gifts, talents, and abilities that You have endowed them with that they may fulfill their God-given destiny. In Jesus' name, I pray. Amen.

> If any of you lacks wisdom, let him ask of God, who gives to
> all liberally and without reproach, and it will be given to him.
>
> JAMES 1:5 (NKJV)

PRAYERFUL REFLECTION FOR ALL OTHERS
Lord, Your Word declares that You are no respecter of persons; and just as You knew Jeremiah before he was formed in the womb and

---

Ephesians 2:10 (NLT)
For we are God's masterpiece. He has created us anew in Christ Jesus,
so that we can do the good things He planned for us long ago.

---

called and appointed him to be a prophet to the nations, You also knew me before I was formed in my mother's womb and have called and appointed me to do great and mighty exploits on earth.

Because this calling was upon my life even as I was being fashioned, I realize that my natural behaviors as a youth reflected the motivational gift that You placed on the inside of me. Lord, I know that this gifting is to enable me to fulfill Your will for my life; and I pray now that by Your Spirit I will recall the innermost desires and passions of my youth. It is my prayer, Father, that You will bring back to my remembrance the goals, dreams, and desires that I had as a young child before life's experiences impacted my steps.

I thank You Lord that I will remember significant things from my past to enable me to operate in my purpose. May this new knowledge awaken a renewed sense of direction and meaning to my life as I take great steps toward gaining full revelation of my God-given purpose. In Jesus' name, I pray. Amen.

DAY 2: ACTION PLAN

 Please use the *Self-Assessment Workbook* as needed to complete the following items in your action plan.

For Parents or Guardians

1. Spend time before the Lord in prayer and ask Him to reveal things to you about your children that will enable you to help them determine their purpose. (John 16:13)
2. Begin to more carefully observe your child in natural environments, paying particular attention to his behaviors and

---

Proverbs 16:9 (AMP)
A man's mind plans his way, but the Lord directs his steps and makes them sure.

---

tendencies at a heightened level. Write down your observations here in your journal.

3. Write down your observations, including your child's habits, behaviors, thoughts, and so forth, here in your journal. Have your child journal as well.
4. Ask your child questions and observe his actions and behaviors to help you to narrow down his motivational gift.
5. Have your child share his innermost dreams and desires. Place them here in your journal. Have your child journal in his journal as well.
6. Observe your child's hobbies and interests to gain insight into his natural abilities and talents.
7. Expose your child to a wide array of new experiences and occupations.
8. Demonstrate Christian character qualities and morality before your child.
9. Place your child in an educational environment that will promote his gifts, talents, and abilities.
10. Set aside time alone with your child to better understand his interests, thoughts, and goals.
11. Assist your child in finding job shadowing, internships, and part-time work in his areas of interest.
12. Assist your child in seeking excellent mentors.
13. Encourage your child to participate in civic and volunteer activities.
14. Be a person who understands and is committed to the greater good.

Jeremiah 1:5
Before I formed you in the womb, I knew you; Before you were born,
I sanctified you; I ordained you a prophet to the nations.

For All Others

1. Spend time in prayer and ask the Holy Spirit to reveal things from your childhood that will assist you in identifying your life purpose. (John 14:26) Make notes here in your journal of the revelations you receive.

2. Take time to reflect upon what you remember being interested in performing while growing up and write it down here in your journal.

3. Prayerfully think about what you enjoyed most as a child, what you were passionate about, and what excited you the most. Place this information here in your journal.

4. Write down your childhood dreams here in your journal.

5. Reflect upon early work, civic, and volunteer experiences. Think about the ones you enjoyed doing the most and write down what made those opportunities more memorable than others here in your journal. Note the areas you excelled in.

6. Ask your parents, siblings, other relatives, and close family friends about your behaviors and interests as a child. Write down their observations here in your journal.

7. Reflect on your education, training, and other experiences to identify your natural gifts and abilities and to determine whether you developed your gifts into talents.

8. As a child, which single occupation did you want to become more than any other and why did you choose it over others? Write that occupation here in your journal and prayerfully take it before God to see if it is His will for your life if you did not pursue it.

Proverbs 4:7
Wisdom is the principal thing; Therefore get wisdom.
And in all your getting, get understanding.

DAY 2: JOURNAL

_____

_____

_____

_____

_____

_____

_____

_____

_____

_____

_____

_____

_____

Psalm 139:14
I will praise You, for I am fearfully and wonderfully made,
Marvelous are Your works, and that my soul knows very well.

_____

Mark 9:23
All things are possible to him
who believes.

Colossians 3:23
And whatever you do,
do it heartily, as to the Lord, and not to men.

DAY TWO : PAGE 22

_____

_____

_____

_____

_____

_____

_____

_____

_____

_____

_____

_____

_____

_____

_____

Jeremiah 29:11
For I know the thoughts that I think toward you, says the LORD;
thoughts of peace and not of evil, to give you a future and a hope.

_____

_____

_____

_____

_____

_____

_____

_____

_____

_____

_____

_____

_____

_____

Psalm 35:27 (NLT)
But give great joy to those who have stood with me in my defense.
Let them continually say, "Great is the LORD, who enjoys helping his servant."

Job 36:11
*If they obey and serve Him, They shall spend their days
in prosperity, And their years in pleasures.*

_____

_____

_____

_____

_____

_____

_____

_____

_____

_____

_____

_____

_____

_____

Psalm 37:23
The steps of a good man are ordered by the LORD,
And He delights in his way.

———

DAY TWO : PAGE 26

PURPOSE

DAY THREE

Day 3 focuses on the importance of determining your ruling passion and allowing it to govern your decisions on educational training, activities, and jobs that you undertake during young adulthood. God placed a ruling passion in you that reflects your innermost being. Uncovering your ruling passion is pivotal in discovering your God-given purpose.

3

Narrowing Your Focus – Young Adulthood

- Ideally, by young adulthood, you should have determined your God-given motivational gift.

- A ruling passion is an intense, overwhelming, driving, heartfelt, deep-seated interest.

- Based upon your childhood interests, abilities, gifts, and talents, you should have identified your ruling passion.

- God placed a ruling passion on the inside of you, and identifying it is the key to discovering your purpose and life work.

- Your ruling passion should govern your choice of jobs, and more notably your life work.

- Life work is the work you dedicate your life to and the work that allows you to attain your greatest success.

- Civic duty, volunteer activities, mentors, hobbies, and interests should be selected based on your ruling passion.

- By beginning your life work, you will allow your natural, God-given gifting and abilities to flourish and develop, thereby increasing the likelihood of your success and prosperity.

- Undertaking your life work puts you in a position to receive a greater blessing from the Lord, enjoy a fuller and more satisfied life, and please God.

 See Day Three: Narrowing Your Focus — Young Adulthood in *How to Discover Your Purpose in 10 Days.*

PRAYERFUL REFLECTION

Lord, I realize my most fervent and enthusiastic interests represent my ruling passion. I pray now that You will help me to identify it that I may begin to select the jobs and civic activities that will allow me to make my innermost dreams a reality.

I thank You now that as I identify my ruling passion, I will begin to see the life work I have been anointed to complete. I know that once I start my life work and begin pursuing my ruling passion, I

Jeremiah 33:3
Call to Me, and I will answer you,
and show you great and mighty things, which you do not know.

will have immense satisfaction and an increased ability to achieve maximum results in my work. I thank You in advance, Lord, for this powerful awakening and revelation. I purpose to faithfully execute my life work as it is revealed to me. In Jesus' name, I pray. Amen.

DAY 3: ACTION PLAN

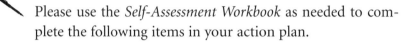 Please use the *Self-Assessment Workbook* as needed to complete the following items in your action plan.

1. Pray and ask God to show you how to narrow and mature in your purpose. (James 1:5)
2. Perform the self-assessments for Day 3.
   a. Talents and Abilities
   b. Job Skills
   c. Work Environment
   d. Work Preferences
3. Identify your ruling passion and write it here in your journal.
4. Pray and ask God to help you identify your life work.
5. Select job assignments that match your talents, skills, and abilities.
6. Identify the type of volunteer actvities that will help you further identify your life work and life purpose.
7. Identify and engage mentors who will help you determine your purpose.
8. Develop hobbies that give insight and will allow you to mature in your natural talents and abilities.

Philippians 4:13
I can do all things through Christ who strengthens me.

DAY 3: JOURNAL

Matthew 21:22
And whatever things you ask in prayer,
believing, you will receive.

_____

_____

_____

_____

_____

_____

_____

_____

_____

_____

_____

_____

_____

Proverbs 16:3 (NLT)
*Commit your work to the LORD, and then
your plans will succeed.*

DAY THREE : PAGE 33

_____

_____

_____

_____

_____

_____

_____

_____

_____

_____

_____

_____

_____

_____

_____

Psalm 16:11
You will show me the path of life; In Your presence is fullness of joy;
At Your right hand are pleasures forevermore.

_____

_____

_____

_____

_____

_____

_____

_____

_____

_____

_____

_____

_____

_____

_____

_____

Ephesians 2:10 (NLT)
For we are God's masterpiece. He has created us anew in Christ Jesus,
so that we can do the good things He planned for us long ago.

_____

_____

_____

_____

_____

_____

_____

_____

_____

_____

_____

_____

_____

Proverbs 16:9 (AMP)
*A man's mind plans his way, but the Lord directs
his steps and makes them sure.*

DAY THREE : PAGE 36

Jeremiah 1:5
Before I formed you in the womb, I knew you; Before you were born,
I sanctified you; I ordained you a prophet to the nations.

DAY THREE : PAGE 37

_____

_____

_____

_____

_____

_____

_____

_____

_____

_____

_____

_____

_____

_____

_____

Proverbs 4:7
Wisdom is the principal thing; Therefore get wisdom.
And in all your getting, get understanding.

_____

PURPOSE

DAY FOUR

Day 4 is the day of breakthrough! It reveals many of the obstacles that may arise along your pathway to purpose. There are countless reasons why you may get diverted, distracted, or thwarted from your pathway to purpose. Day 4 helps you locate yourself, make the necessary adjustments, and begin operating in your purpose.

4

DAY FOUR

Obstacles on the Pathway to Purpose

- You will face obstacles along your pathway to purpose.

- Some of the distractions that arise in your life that cause you to lose focus are self-determined and may be avoided by a change in behavior.

- You can overcome the obstacles that arise along your pathway to purpose by repenting of the mistakes you made in the past and making a decision to research and apply God's Word and use His solutions to the problem to have victory.

- God has provided you with the grace necessary to overcome any hindrance that would impede you from fulfilling your purpose.

- Know that Satan will continually try to knock you off of your path to purpose. But remember: *he* is a defeated foe.

> Little children, you are of God [you belong to Him] and have [already] defeated and overcome them [the agents of the antichrist], because He Who lives in you is greater (mightier) than he who is in the world.
>
> 1 JOHN 4:4 (AMP)

- As a believer, you have the power of God to conquer any stumbling block placed in your pathway.

> But thanks be to God, who gives us the victory through our Lord Jesus Christ.
>
> 1 CORINTHIANS 15:57 (NKJV)

- Understand that although you may fall, you must repent, learn from the mistake, and make a decision to get back on your pathway to purpose.

> For a righteous man may fall seven times and rise again, But the wicked shall fall by calamity.
>
> PROVERBS 24:16 (NKJV)

Psalm 139:14
I will praise You, for I am fearfully and wonderfully made, Marvelous are Your works, and that my soul knows very well.

See Day Four: Obstacles on the Pathway to Purpose in *How to Discover Your Purpose in 10 Days.*

PRAYERFUL REFLECTION

Lord, I know that You have commanded us to remain free from any bondages that would stop us from doing Your will and I thank You that whom the Son has set free is free indeed. Therefore, I am, right now, free from my past and any detrimental habits that have hindered me from fulfilling my purpose. I make a decision to follow Your Word.

I repent and ask for Your forgiveness for making ungodly decisions, harboring bitterness and resentment towards others for injustices done against me, having destructive habits, being unequally yoked in my relationships, and for allowing the negative aspects of my past to prevent me from moving forward into the great and mighty things You foreordained for me. (Philippians 3:13-15) I thank You, Father, for forgiving me and I accept Your forgiveness. I also forgive myself; and I commit to learn and apply Your Word to my life from this day forward, to be a doer of the Word of God. (James 1:22) In Jesus' name, I pray. Amen.

DAY 4: ACTION PLAN

Please use the *Self-Assessment Workbook* as needed to complete the following items in your action plan.

Mark 9:23
*All things are possible to him
who believes.*

As you fulfill God's will concerning your life, you must stay on your pathway to purpose and overcome any obstacles that would attempt to hinder you. You would be well guided to complete the following steps.

1. Give your life to the Lord or rededicate yourself back to Him. If you have already done this, consecrate yourself to the Lord to have Him help you.
2. Forgive others for the injustices that they may have done against you — intentionally and/or unintentionally.
3. Spend time in prayer to get God's will and wisdom on how to handle situations.
4. Find out what God's Word has to say about the matter and make a decision to begin to apply His principles immediately.
5. Stop destructive habits and stop making excuses for neglecting what you know you should be doing. Be led by the Spirit of God and wholeheartedly seek to do His will.
6. Remove yourself from any ungodly situations. Refrain from getting involved in activities that tempt you to engage in and distract you from doing God's will.
7. Get out of ungodly relationships. Begin to surround yourself with godly influences. Get involved in your local church.
8. Refrain from meditating or thinking about the negative events of the past. Move on. Once you accept Jesus Christ into your heart as your Lord and Savior, you are a new creation.

Colossians 3:23
And whatever you do,
do it heartily, as to the Lord, and not to men.

Therefore, if anyone is in Christ, he is a new creation; old
things have passed away; behold, all things have become new.

2 CORINTHIANS 5:17 (NKJV)

9. Going forward, if you miss the mark in an area and find
yourself off your pathway, repent and immediately get back
on track. Remember, no matter how many times you miss
it, God loves you and He is always ready and willing to forgive you. He wants to see you victorious in every situation.

If we confess our sins, He is faithful and just to forgive us our
sins and to cleanse us from all unrighteousness.

1 JOHN 1:9 (NKJV)

10. If you find yourself off your path to purpose, redirect yourself on to the right road:
    a. Repent for the mistake
    b. Get God's Word on the situation and immediately
       apply His principles
    c. Forgive yourself and all others involved
    d. Find an excellent mentor
    e. Acquire the appropriate education and job training
       needed to fulfill your purpose
    f. Read books, trade journals, and manuals that provide
       the information that you need

Jeremiah 29:11
For I know the thoughts that I think toward you, says the LORD;
thoughts of peace and not of evil, to give you a future and a hope.

DAY 4: JOURNAL

_____

_____

_____

_____

_____

_____

_____

_____

_____

_____

_____

_____

Psalm 35:27 (NLT)
But give great joy to those who have stood with me in my defense.
Let them continually say, "Great is the LORD, who enjoys helping his servant."

_____

_____

_____

_____

_____

_____

_____

_____

_____

_____

_____

_____

_____

Job 36:11
*If they obey and serve Him, They shall spend their days
in prosperity, And their years in pleasures.*

———————

Psalm 37:23
The steps of a good man are ordered by the LORD,
And He delights in his way.

_____

_____

_____

_____

_____

_____

_____

_____

_____

_____

_____

_____

_____

Jeremiah 33:3
Call to Me, and I will answer you,
and show you great and mighty things, which you do not know.

_____

_____

_____

_____

_____

_____

_____

_____

_____

_____

_____

_____

_____

_____

_____

_____

_____

Philippians 4:13
*I can do all things through Christ
who strengthens me.*

_____

_____

_____

_____

_____

_____

_____

_____

_____

_____

_____

_____

_____

_____

Matthew 21:22
And whatever things you ask in prayer,
believing, you will receive.

_____

_____

_____

_____

_____

_____

_____

_____

_____

_____

_____

_____

_____

_____

Proverbs 16:3 (NLT)
*Commit your work to the LORD, and then
your plans will succeed.*

$\mathcal{P}$URPOSE

D·A·Y   F·I·V·E

In Day 5, the motivational gifts are introduced and the motivational gift of the Perceiver is discussed. God has called the Perceiver to intercede on the behalf of others and distinguish between right and wrong.

5

God's Unique Motivational Gifts – Introduction / Perceiver

- God has granted each of us a different vantage point from which we view life. It is found in Romans 12:6-8 and is known as the motivational gift.

- There are seven motivational gifts in operation.

- God has endowed you with one motivational gift, although you may exhibit characteristics of the other motivational gifts.

- All gifts are vital to every area of your life, including your family, church, and workplace.

- Knowing your motivational gift is a major key in identifying your purpose.

- Understanding the characteristics of the motivational gifts is critical to improving your relationships with others.

 See Day Five: God's Unique Motivational Gifts — Introduction/Perceiver in *How to Discover Your Purpose in 10 Days.*

PRAYERFUL REFLECTION

Lord, I thank You for the unique way that You have wired me. I know that You have equipped me with certain abilities, talents, and gifts to accomplish a great and mighty task upon earth. I thank You that in order to fulfill my purpose, I have been endowed with a motivational gift that determines my outlook on life and my response to situations. I thank You that this knowledge will further enable me to identify my purpose while revealing my strengths and weaknesses so that I am able to interact with and understand myself and others at a higher level. In Jesus' name, I pray. Amen.

PRAYERFUL REFLECTION FOR THE PERCEIVER MOTIVATIONAL GIFT

Lord, I thank You for creating me in Your very own image with a strong intolerance for wrong; and I thank You for anointing me with the ability to discern between right and wrong at a high level.

Father, I accept this gift from You. I realize that the gifting You have placed on the inside of me is of vital importance in carrying

---

Psalm 16:11
You will show me the path of life; In Your presence is fullness of joy;
At Your right hand are pleasures forevermore.

---

out Your plans and purposes on earth. Therefore, I thank You for gifting me with a natural ability to judge character, make decisions easily, and implement policies and procedures well.

I count it an honor and a privilege that You have empowered me to serve as Your agent for moral and ethical integrity on earth, while calling me to intercede on behalf of others that they may fulfill Your will.

Now that I know how I am wired, I commit myself to developing and maturing in my gift. From this day forward, I will seek jobs, volunteer activities, and hobbies that will further enable me to mature in my gifting.

I realize that there are strengths and weaknesses inherent in each of the motivational gifts. Therefore, I will strive to maximize my strengths and temper my weaknesses by working to cultivate the positive attributes of the other motivational gifts into my life.

I value other people's perspectives and as I continue learning about their motivational gifts, I will embrace them, for I know each of us has a unique responsibility from You. In Jesus' name, I pray. Amen.

DAY 5: PERCEIVER ACTION PLAN

 Please use the *Self-Assessment Workbook* as needed to complete the following items in your action plan.

Section A
1. Perform the Perceiver self-assessment.
2. Attempt to determine if you are a Perceiver motivational gift.

Ephesians 2:10 (NLT)
For we are God's masterpiece. He has created us anew in Christ Jesus, so that we can do the good things He planned for us long ago.

---

    a. If yes, continue to section B, question 3 and complete the steps. (Skip section C.)

    b. If no, continue to section C, question 12 and complete the steps.

    c. If unsure, continue to complete all sections concerning the remaining motivational gifts (see Days 5-8) and complete all motivational gift self-assessments.

Section B

3. If you have successfully determined that you are a Perceiver, congratulations! You have been wired by God to perceive, recognize, and distinguish between right and wrong. That is a blessing! The identification of your motivational gift is very helpful in determining your God-given purpose.

4. Pray and thank God for how He made you; for you have been fearfully and wonderfully made. God needed you to be this way to fulfill His plans and purposes for your life.

5. Decide to accept yourself as God made you. Many people don't accept the way God made them. They desire to become another motivational gift rather than who God made them to be. That will slow up your process of development.

6. Review the characteristics of the Perceiver motivational gift and begin to observe your motivational gift in operation in your life. Write your observations here in your journal.

    a. Observe why and how you make decisions.

    b. Observe how you respond to situations.

    c. Observe your thought processes.

    d. Observe your natural interactions with people.

    e. If your behaviors don't line up with the general charac-

---

Proverbs 16:9 (AMP)
A man's mind plans his way, but the Lord directs
his steps and makes them sure.

---

teristics, re-evaluate yourself to determine if you need to re-identify your motivational gift.

Remember: You do not have to perfectly match every characteristic in order to be that motivational gift.

7. Have those closest to you (spouse, parents, children, close friend) confirm your motivational gift.
   a. Have those close to you review the characteristics of the Perceiver and confirm whether you line up with them.
   b. Those close to you will have an independent opinion of how you really act.
   c. If you don't line up, start over in the identification process.
8. After confirming your gift, determine your strengths and begin to develop them at a higher level. List them here in your journal.
   a. Go back and review the abilities, skills, and interests self-assessments and see if there is a pattern in line with your motivational gift.
   b. Have a heightened awareness of things you do well and that come easily for you.
   c. Begin to develop your strengths through mentorship, formal study or training, and/or home study, including tapes and books.
9. Recognize your weaknesses and place them here in your journal. These are the areas you will want to temper as you mature.
   a. Determine your weaknesses in social interaction and learn to temper or develop in those areas.
   b. Recognize the areas in which you are not naturally

Jeremiah 1:5

Before I formed you in the womb, I knew you; Before you were born, I sanctified you; I ordained you a prophet to the nations.

---

gifted and determine how to delegate and defer to others for help.

10. Begin to identify job and work situations in which your motivational gift can be fully expressed.

    a. You may already be in the best situation to express your motivational gift.

    b. You may need to see your present job from a different perspective.

    c. It may mean slightly adjusting your present job responsibilities and duties.

    d. You may need to believe God to be reassigned to a new position in the company or to find a new job. If this is the case, be patient and allow God to direct your steps.

11. Begin to allow your gift to be expressed in your service to other people.

    a. Serve God and the body of Christ in areas that are supported by your motivational gift.

    b. Serve your family, friends, and community, and perform civic duties using your motivational gift.

Section C

If you do not possess the motivational gift of Perceiver, consider the following.

12. Identify those in your circle of family and friends who possess this motivational gift.

_____   _____

_____   _____

Proverbs 4:7
Wisdom is the principal thing; Therefore get wisdom.
And in all your getting, get understanding.

_____

13. Study the differences in patterns and behavior between the Perceiver and yourself.
    a. The ability to understand others and effectively interact with people is a fundamental key to success.
    b. Think about times you could have misunderstood a Perceiver because you did not understand the gift.
    c. Purpose to attempt to understand the Perceiver rather than judging them.
    d. Learn to accept and not reject the perspective of the Perceiver even though it is different from your own.
    e. Pray and ask God to give you wisdom on how to properly interact with the Perceiver motivational gift.
14. Study the strong characteristics of the Perceiver motivational gift and build these characteristics into your behavior patterns.
    a. Learn the positive behaviors of the Perceiver.
    b. Avoid the negative behaviors of the Perceiver.
15. Determine ways to utilize or rely on a Perceiver to help you accomplish your goals and tasks.
    a. Determine the ways someone of this motivational gift can help compensate for your weaknesses.
    b. Determine if you should completely delegate a task to the Perceiver or just ask for advice or help.

Psalm 139:14
I will praise You, for I am fearfully and wonderfully made,
Marvelous are Your works, and that my soul knows very well.

c. Learn to embrace each motivational gift for the unique wisdom and perspective toward life that God gave them.

DAY 5: JOURNAL

Colossians 3:23
And whatever you do,
do it heartily, as to the Lord, and not to men.

DAY FIVE : PAGE 63

_____

_____

_____

_____

_____

_____

_____

_____

_____

_____

_____

_____

_____

_____

Jeremiah 29:11
For I know the thoughts that I think toward you, says the LORD;
thoughts of peace and not of evil, to give you a future and a hope.

_____

DAY FIVE : PAGE 64

_____

_____

_____

_____

_____

_____

_____

_____

_____

_____

_____

_____

_____

_____

Psalm 35:27 (NLT)
But give great joy to those who have stood with me in my defense.
Let them continually say, "Great is the LORD, who enjoys helping his servant."

_____

_____

_____

_____

_____

_____

_____

_____

_____

_____

_____

_____

_____

_____

_____

Job 36:11
If they obey and serve Him, They shall spend their days
in prosperity, And their years in pleasures.

_____

DAY FIVE : PAGE 66

Psalm 37:23
The steps of a good man are ordered by the LORD,
And He delights in his way.

Jeremiah 33:3
Call to Me, and I will answer you,
and show you great and mighty things, which you do not know.

PURPOSE

DAY SIX

In Day 6, the motivational gifts of Server and Teacher are revealed. God has called the Server to perform the practical needs of others, while the Teacher has been anointed by God to manage and disseminate information.

6

God's Unique Motivational Gifts – Server / Teacher

SERVER

- God created the gift of Server to perform the practical needs of people.

- Servers receive joy from assisting others and usually have a keen ability to sense what people need.

- Servers love to be around people and typically have a high energy level.

- Servers prefer doing multiple tasks simultaneously and short-range projects to meet immediate needs.

TEACHER
- God created the gift of Teacher to manage and disseminate information.

- Teachers usually enjoy learning and reading nonfiction.

- Teachers love to give information and tend to present information in a systematic, organized format.

- Teachers are usually self-disciplined and enjoy complex problem solving.

 See Day Six: God's Unique Motivational Gifts — Server/ Teacher in *How to Discover Your Purpose in 10 Days*.

PRAYERFUL REFLECTION FOR THE SERVER MOTIVATIONAL GIFT
Lord, I thank You for creating me in Your own image with a strong passion for serving others; and I thank You for anointing me with the ability to discern what people need.

Father, I accept this gift. I realize that the gifting You have placed on the inside of me is vital in carrying out Your plans and purposes on earth. Therefore, I thank You for gifting me with a natural ability to assist others, display hospitality, and work well with others.

I count it an honor and a privilege that You have empowered me to serve people and to perform multiple tasks simultaneously so that I am able to get a lot accomplished.

Now that I know how I am wired, I commit myself to developing

Philippians 4:13
*I can do all things through Christ
who strengthens me.*

and maturing in my gift. From this day forward, I will seek jobs, volunteer activities, and hobbies that will further enable me to mature in my gifting.

I realize that there are strengths and weaknesses inherent in each of the motivational gifts. Therefore, I will strive to maximize my strengths and temper my weaknesses by working to cultivate the positive attributes of the other motivational gifts into my life.

I value other people's perspectives, and as I continue learning about their motivational gifts, I will embrace them, for I know each of us has a unique responsibility from You. In Jesus' name, I pray. Amen.

PRAYERFUL REFLECTION FOR THE TEACHER MOTIVATIONAL GIFT

Lord, I thank You for creating me in Your own image with the ability to think long-range; and I thank You for anointing me to gather, process, and disseminate information.

Father, I accept this gift. I realize that the gifting You have placed on the inside of me is vital in carrying out Your plans and purposes on earth. Therefore, I thank You for gifting me with a natural ability to study, share information, and solve complex problems.

I count it an honor and a privilege that You have empowered me with a love for reading, the ability to make good decisions, and the desire to serve people through the dissemination of vital information.

Now that I know how I am wired, I commit myself to developing and maturing in my gift. From this day forward, I will seek jobs, volunteer activities, and hobbies that will further enable me to mature in my gifting.

Matthew 21:22
*And whatever things you ask in prayer,
believing, you will receive.*

I realize that there are strengths and weaknesses inherent in each of the motivational gifts. Therefore, I will strive to maximize my strengths and temper my weaknesses by working to cultivate the positive attributes of the other motivational gifts into my life.

I value other people's perspectives, and as I continue learning about their motivational gifts, I will embrace them, for I know each of us has a unique responsibility from You. In Jesus' name, I pray. Amen.

DAY 6: SERVER ACTION PLAN

Please use the *Self-Assessment Workbook* as needed to complete the following items in your action plan.

Section A
1. Perform the Server self-assessment.
2. Attempt to determine if you are a Server motivational gift.
   a. If yes, continue to section B, question 3 and complete the steps. (Skip section C.)
   b. If no, continue to section C, question 12 and complete the steps.
   c. If unsure, continue to complete all sections concerning the remaining motivational gifts (see Days 5-8) and complete all motivational gift self-assessments.

Section B
3. If you have successfully determined that you are a Server, congratulations! You have been wired by God to perform the practical needs of others. That is a blessing! The identification

---

Proverbs 16:3 (NLT)
*Commit your work to the LORD, and then
your plans will succeed.*

---

of your motivational gift is very helpful in determining your God-given purpose.

4. Pray and thank God for how He made you; for you have been fearfully and wonderfully made. God needed you to be this way to fulfill His plans and purposes for your life.

5. Decide to accept yourself as God made you. Many people don't accept the way God made them. They desire to become another motivational gift rather than who God made them to be. That will slow up your process of development.

6. Review the characteristics of the Server motivational gift and begin to observe your motivational gift in operation in your life. Write your observations here in your journal.
    a. Observe why and how you make decisions.
    b. Observe how you respond to situations.
    c. Observe your thought processes.
    d. Observe your natural interactions with people.
    e. If your behaviors don't line up with the general characteristics, re-evaluate yourself to determine if you need to re-identify your motivational gift.
    Remember: You do not have to perfectly match every characteristic in order to be that motivational gift.

7. Have those closest to you (spouse, parents, children, close friend) confirm your motivational gift.
    a. Have those close to you review the characteristics of the Server and confirm whether you line up with them.
    b. Those close to you will have an independent opinion of how you really act.
    c. If you don't line up, start over in the identification process.

Psalm 16:11
*You will show me the path of life; In Your presence is fullness of joy;
At Your right hand are pleasures forevermore.*

---

8. After confirming your gift, determine your strengths and begin to develop them at a higher level. List them here in your journal.

    a. Go back and review the abilities, skills, and interests self-assessments and see if there is a pattern in line with your motivational gift.

    b. Have a heightened awareness of things you do well and that come easily for you.

    c. Begin to develop your strengths through mentorship, formal study or training, and/or home study, including tapes and books.

9. Recognize your weaknesses and place them here in your journal. These are the areas you will want to temper as you mature.

    a. Determine your weaknesses in social interaction and learn to temper or develop in those areas.

    b. Recognize the areas in which you are not naturally gifted and determine how to delegate and defer to others for help.

10. Begin to identify job and work situations in which your motivational gift can be fully expressed.

    a. You may already be in the best situation to express your motivational gift.

    b. You may need to see your present job from a different perspective.

    c. It may mean slightly adjusting your present job responsibilities and duties.

    d. You may need to believe God to be reassigned to a new

Ephesians 2:10 (NLT)
For we are God's masterpiece. He has created us anew in Christ Jesus, so that we can do the good things He planned for us long ago.

---

position in the company or to find a new job. If this is the case, be patient and allow God to direct your steps.

11. Begin to allow your gift to be expressed in your service to other people.
    a. Serve God and the body of Christ in areas that are supported by your motivational gift.
    b. Serve your family, friends, and community, and perform civic duties using your motivational gift.

Section C

If you do not possess the motivational gift of Server, consider the following.

12. Identify those in your circle of family and friends who possess this motivational gift.

_____	_____
_____	_____
_____	_____
_____	_____

13. Study the differences in patterns and behavior between the Server and yourself.
    a. The ability to understand others and effectively interact with people is a fundamental key to success.
    b. Think about times you could have misunderstood a Server because you did not understand the gift.

Proverbs 16:9 (AMP)
A man's mind plans his way, but the Lord directs his steps and makes them sure.

     c. Purpose to attempt to understand the Server rather than judging them.

     d. Learn to accept and not reject the perspective of the Server even though it is different from your own.

     e. Pray and ask God to give you wisdom on how to properly interact with the Server motivational gift.

14. Study the strong characteristics of the Server motivational gift and build these characteristics into your behavior patterns.

     a. Learn the positive behaviors of the Server.

     b. Avoid the negative behaviors of the Server.

15. Determine ways to utilize or rely on a Server to help you accomplish your goals and tasks.

     a. Determine the ways someone of this motivational gift can help compensate for your weaknesses.

     b. Determine if you should completely delegate a task to the Server or just ask for advice or help.

     c. Learn to embrace each motivational gift for the unique wisdom and perspective toward life that God gave them.

DAY 6: TEACHER ACTION PLAN

Please use the *Self-Assessment Workbook* as needed to complete the following items in your action plan.

Section A

1. Perform the Teacher self-assessment.
2. Attempt to determine if you are a Teacher motivational gift.

Jeremiah 1:5
Before I formed you in the womb, I knew you; Before you were born, I sanctified you; I ordained you a prophet to the nations.

---

    a. If yes, continue to section B, question 3 and complete the steps. (Skip section C.)

    b. If no, continue to section C, question 12 and complete the steps.

    c. If unsure, continue to complete all sections concerning the remaining motivational gifts (see Days 5-8) and complete all motivational gift self-assessments.

Section B

3. If you have successfully determined that you are a Teacher, congratulations! You have been wired by God to disseminate and manage information. That is a blessing! The identification of your motivational gift is very helpful in determining your God-given purpose.

4. Pray and thank God for how He made you; for you have been fearfully and wonderfully made. God needed you to be this way to fulfill His plans and purposes for your life.

5. Decide to accept yourself as God made you. Many people don't accept the way God made them. They desire to become another motivational gift rather than who God made them to be. That will slow up your process of development.

6. Review the characteristics of the Teacher motivational gift and begin to observe your motivational gift in operation in your life. Write your observations here in your journal.

    a. Observe why and how you make decisions.

    b. Observe how you respond to situations.

    c. Observe your thought processes.

    d. Observe your natural interactions with people.

Proverbs 4:7
Wisdom is the principal thing; Therefore get wisdom.
And in all your getting, get understanding.

---

    e. If your behaviors don't line up with the general char-
acteristics, re-evaluate yourself to determine if you need
to re-identify your motivational gift.

Remember: You do not have to perfectly match every
characteristic in order to be that motivational gift.

7. Have those closest to you (spouse, parents, children, close
friend) confirm your motivational gift.

    a. Have those close to you review the characteristics of the
Teacher and confirm whether you line up with them.

    b. Those close to you will have an independent opinion
of how you really act.

    c. If you don't line up, start over in the identification
process.

8. After confirming your gift, determine your strengths and
begin to develop them at a higher level. List them here in your
journal.

    a. Go back and review the abilities, skills, and interests
self-assessments and see if there is a pattern in line with
your motivational gift.

    b. Have a heightened awareness of things you do well
and that come easily for you.

    c. Begin to develop your strengths through mentorship,
formal study or training, and/or home study, including tapes and books.

9. Recognize your weaknesses and place them here in your journal. These are the areas you will want to temper as you mature.

    a. Determine your weaknesses in social interaction and
learn to temper or develop in those areas.

    b. Recognize the areas in which you are not naturally

Psalm 139:14
I will praise You, for I am fearfully and wonderfully made,
Marvelous are Your works, and that my soul knows very well.

---

gifted and determine how to delegate and defer to others for help.

10. Begin to identify job and work situations in which your motivational gift can be fully expressed.

    a. You may already be in the best situation to express your motivational gift.

    b. You may need to see your present job from a different perspective.

    c. It may mean slightly adjusting your present job responsibilities and duties.

    d. You may need to believe God to be reassigned to a new position in the company or to find a new job. If this is the case, be patient and allow God to direct your steps.

11. Begin to allow your gift to be expressed in your service to other people.

    a. Serve God and the body of Christ in areas that are supported by your motivational gift.

    b. Serve your family, friends, and community, and perform civic duties using your motivational gift.

Section C

If you do not possess the motivational gift of Teacher, consider the following.

12. Identify those in your circle of family and friends who possess this motivational gift.

Mark 9:23
All things are possible to him who believes.

_____   _____

_____   _____

13. Study the differences in patterns and behavior between the Teacher and yourself.
    a. The ability to understand others and effectively interact with people is a fundamental key to success.
    b. Think about times you could have misunderstood a Teacher because you did not understand the gift.
    c. Purpose to attempt to understand the Teacher rather than judging them.
    d. Learn to accept and not reject the perspective of the Teacher even though it is different from your own.
    e. Pray and ask God to give you wisdom on how to properly interact with the Teacher motivational gift.
14. Study the strong characteristics of the Teacher motivational gift and build these characteristics into your behavior patterns.
    a. Learn the positive behaviors of the Teacher.
    b. Avoid the negative behaviors of the Teacher.
15. Determine ways to utilize or rely on a Teacher to help you accomplish your goals and tasks.
    a. Determine the ways someone of this motivational gift can help compensate for your weaknesses.
    b. Determine if you should completely delegate a task to the Teacher or just ask for advice or help.
    c. Learn to embrace each motivational gift for the unique wisdom and perspective toward life that God gave them.

_____

Colossians 3:23
And whatever you do,
do it heartily, as to the Lord, and not to men.

_____

DAY 6: JOURNAL

_____

_____

_____

_____

_____

_____

_____

_____

_____

_____

_____

_____

_____

_____

Jeremiah 29:11
For I know the thoughts that I think toward you, says the LORD;
thoughts of peace and not of evil, to give you a future and a hope.

_____

_____

_____

_____

_____

_____

_____

_____

_____

_____

_____

_____

_____

_____

Psalm 35:27 (NLT)
But give great joy to those who have stood with me in my defense.
Let them continually say, "Great is the LORD, who enjoys helping his servant."

_____

_____

_____

_____

_____

_____

_____

_____

_____

_____

_____

_____

Psalm 37:23
The steps of a good man are ordered by the LORD,
And He delights in his way.

DAY SIX : PAGE 86

_____

_____

_____

_____

_____

_____

_____

_____

_____

_____

_____

_____

_____

_____

Jeremiah 33:3
Call to Me, and I will answer you,
and show you great and mighty things, which you do not know.

_____

_____

_____

_____

_____

_____

_____

_____

_____

_____

_____

_____

_____

_____

_____

_____

Philippians 4:13
I can do all things through Christ
who strengthens me.

_____

DAY SIX : PAGE 88

PURPOSE
DAY SEVEN

In Day 7, the motivational gifts of Exhorter and Giver are uncovered. God has called the Exhorter to encourage and build people up, while the Giver has been anointed by God to mobilize resources for the aid and benefit of others.

7

God's Unique Motivational Gifts – Exhorter / Giver

EXHORTER

- God created the Exhorter to help people live up to their full potential by endowing them with a keen ability to encourage and build people up.

- Exhorters tend to be talkative, outspoken people.

- Exhorters have positive attitudes and are usually nonjudgmental.

- Exhorters like to practically apply information and they are usually considered how-to people.

GIVER

- God created Givers to mobilize resources for the aid and benefit of others.

- Givers tend to be outgoing and sensitive to the unmet needs of others.

- Givers enjoy entertaining and manage their finances wisely.

- Givers are excellent negotiators with a natural aptitude for business.

 See Day Seven: God's Unique Motivational Gifts — Exhorter/ Giver in *How to Discover Your Purpose in 10 Days.*

PRAYERFUL REFLECTION FOR THE EXHORTER MOTIVATIONAL GIFT

Lord, I thank You for creating me in Your own image with a concern for Your people that they live up to their God-given potential; and I thank You for anointing me to communicate well.

Father, I accept this gift. I realize that the gifting You have placed inside of me is vital in carrying out Your plans and purposes on earth. Therefore, I thank You for gifting me with a natural ability to implement plans, give constructive and helpful advice, and see the good in others.

I count it an honor and a privilege that You have empowered me to build up and exhort people and help people operate in their God-given ability.

Matthew 21:22
And whatever things you ask in prayer,
believing, you will receive.

Now that I know how I am wired, I commit myself to developing and maturing in my gift. From this day forward, I will seek jobs, volunteer activities, and hobbies that will further enable me to mature in my gifting.

I realize that there are strengths and weaknesses inherent in each of the motivational gifts. Therefore, I will strive to maximize my strengths and temper my weaknesses by working to cultivate the positive attributes of the other motivational gifts into my life.

I value other people's perspectives, and as I continue learning about their motivational gifts, I will embrace them, for I know each of us has a unique responsibility from You. In Jesus' name, I pray. Amen.

PRAYERFUL REFLECTION FOR THE GIVER MOTIVATIONAL GIFT

Lord, I thank You for creating me in Your own image with the innate desire to give of my resources, money, belongings, time, and energy to aid people; and I thank You for anointing me to negotiate effectively.

Father, I accept this gift. I realize that the gifting You have placed inside of me is vital in carrying out Your plans and purposes on earth. Therefore, I thank You for gifting me with natural business savvy, an ability to recognize legitimate needs, and the ability to manage money with wisdom and prudence.

I count it an honor and a privilege that You have empowered me to be wise and gregarious in an effort to match resources with needs.

Now that I know how I am wired, I commit myself to developing and maturing in my gift. From this day forward, I will seek

Proverbs 16:3 (NLT)
*Commit your work to the LORD, and then
your plans will succeed.*

jobs, volunteer activities, and hobbies that will further enable me to mature in my gifting.

I realize that there are strengths and weaknesses inherent in each of the motivational gifts. Therefore, I will strive to maximize my strengths and temper my weaknesses by working to cultivate the positive attributes of the other motivational gifts into my life.

I value other people's perspectives, and as I continue learning about their motivational gifts, I will embrace them, for I know each of us has a unique responsibility from You. In Jesus' name, I pray. Amen.

DAY 7: EXHORTER ACTION PLAN

Please use the *Self-Assessment Workbook* as needed to complete the following items in your action plan.

Section A

1. Perform the Exhorter self-assessment.
2. Attempt to determine if you are an Exhorter motivational gift.
   a. If yes, continue to section B, question 3 and complete the steps. (Skip section C.)
   b. If no, continue to section C, question 12 and complete the steps.
   c. If unsure, continue to complete all sections concerning the remaining motivational gifts (see Days 5-8) and complete all motivational gift self-assessments.

Psalm 16:11
You will show me the path of life; In Your presence is fullness of joy;
At Your right hand are pleasures forevermore.

Section B

3. If you have successfully determined that you are an Exhorter, congratulations! You have been wired by God to encourage and build people up. That is a blessing! The identification of your motivational gift is very helpful in determining your God-given purpose.

4. Pray and thank God for how He made you; for you have been fearfully and wonderfully made. God needed you to be this way to fulfill His plans and purposes for your life.

5. Decide to accept yourself as God made you. Many people don't accept the way God made them. They desire to become another motivational gift rather than who God made them to be. That will slow up your process of development.

6. Review the characteristics of the Exhorter motivational gift and begin to observe your motivational gift in operation in your life. Write your observations here in your journal.
   a. Observe why and how you make decisions.
   b. Observe how you respond to situations.
   c. Observe your thought processes.
   d. Observe your natural interactions with people.
   e. If your behaviors don't line up with the general characteristics, re-evaluate yourself to determine if you need to re-identify your motivational gift.
   Remember: You do not have to perfectly match every characteristic in order to be that motivational gift.

7. Have those closest to you (spouse, parents, children, close friend) confirm your motivational gift.
   a. Have those close to you review the characteristics of the Exhorter and confirm whether you line up with them.

Ephesians 2:10 (NLT)
*For we are God's masterpiece. He has created us anew in Christ Jesus,
so that we can do the good things He planned for us long ago.*

---

    b. Those close to you will have an independent opinion of how you really act.

    c. If you don't line up, start over in the identification process.

8. After confirming your gift, determine your strengths and begin to develop them at a higher level. List them here in your journal.

    a. Go back and review the abilities, skills, and interests self-assessments and see if there is a pattern in line with your motivational gift.

    b. Have a heightened awareness of things you do well and that come easily for you.

    c. Begin to develop your strengths through mentorship, formal study or training, and/or home study, including tapes and books.

9. Recognize your weaknesses and place them here in your journal. These are the areas you will want to temper as you mature.

    a. Determine your weaknesses in social interaction and learn to temper or develop in those areas.

    b. Recognize the areas in which you are not naturally gifted and determine how to delegate and defer to others for help.

10. Begin to identify job and work situations in which your motivational gift can be fully expressed.

    a. You may already be in the best situation to express your motivational gift.

    b. You may need to see your present job from a different perspective.

Proverbs 16:9 (AMP)
*A man's mind plans his way, but the Lord directs
his steps and makes them sure.*

---

   c. It may mean slightly adjusting your present job responsibilities and duties.

   d. You may need to believe God to be reassigned to a new position in the company or to find a new job. If this is the case, be patient and allow God to direct your steps.

11. Begin to allow your gift to be expressed in your service to other people.

   a. Serve God and the body of Christ in areas that are supported by your motivational gift.

   b. Serve your family, friends, and community, and perform civic duties using your motivational gift.

Section C

If you do not possess the motivational gift of Exhorter, consider the following.

12. Identify those in your circle of family and friends who possess this motivational gift.

_____   _____

_____   _____

_____   _____

_____

13. Study the differences in patterns and behavior between the Exhorter and yourself.

Jeremiah 1:5
*Before I formed you in the womb, I knew you; Before you were born,
I sanctified you; I ordained you a prophet to the nations.*

    a. The ability to understand others and effectively inter-act with people is a fundamental key to success.

    b. Think about times you could have misunderstood an Exhorter because you did not understand the gift.

    c. Purpose to attempt to understand the Exhorter rather than judging them.

    d. Learn to accept and not reject the perspective of the Exhorter even though it is different from your own.

    e. Pray and ask God to give you wisdom on how to properly interact with the Exhorter motivational gift.

14. Study the strong characteristics of the Exhorter motivational gift and build these characteristics into your behavior patterns.

    a. Learn the positive behaviors of the Exhorter.

    b. Avoid the negative behaviors of the Exhorter.

15. Determine ways to utilize or rely on an Exhorter to help you accomplish your goals and tasks.

    a. Determine the ways someone of this motivational gift can help compensate for your weaknesses.

    b. Determine if you should completely delegate a task to the Exhorter or just ask for advice or help.

    c. Learn to embrace each motivational gift for the unique wisdom and perspective toward life that God gave them.

DAY 7: GIVER ACTION PLAN

Please use the *Self-Assessment Workbook* as needed to complete the following items in your action plan.

Proverbs 4:7
Wisdom is the principal thing; Therefore get wisdom.
And in all your getting, get understanding.

Section A

1. Perform the Giver self-assessment.
2. Attempt to determine if you are a Giver motivational gift.
   a. If yes, continue to section B, question 3 and complete the steps. (Skip section C.)
   b. If no, continue to section C, question 12 and complete the steps.
   c. If unsure, continue to complete all sections concerning the remaining motivational gifts (see Days 5-8) and complete all motivational gift self-assessments.

Section B

3. If you have successfully determined that you are a Giver, congratulations! You have been wired by God to mobilize resources for the aid and benefit of others. That is a blessing! The identification of your motivational gift is very helpful in determining your God-given purpose.
4. Pray and thank God for how He made you; for you have been fearfully and wonderfully made. God needed you to be this way to fulfill His plans and purposes for your life.
5. Decide to accept yourself as God made you. Many people don't accept the way God made them. They desire to become another motivational gift rather than who God made them to be. That will slow up your process of development.
6. Review the characteristics of the Giver motivational gift and begin to observe your motivational gift in operation in your life. Write your observations here in your journal.
   a. Observe why and how you make decisions.
   b. Observe how you respond to situations.

Psalm 139:14
I will praise You, for I am fearfully and wonderfully made.
Marvelous are Your works, and that my soul knows very well.

   c. Observe your thought processes.

   d. Observe your natural interactions with people.

   e. If your behaviors don't line up with the general characteristics, re-evaluate yourself to determine if you need to re-identify your motivational gift.

   Remember: You do not have to perfectly match every characteristic in order to be that motivational gift.

7. Have those closest to you (spouse, parents, children, close friend) confirm your motivational gift.

   a. Have those close to you review the characteristics of the Giver and confirm whether you line up with them.

   b. Those close to you will have an independent opinion of how you really act.

   c. If you don't line up, start over in the identification process.

8. After confirming your gift, determine your strengths and begin to develop them at a higher level. List them here in your journal.

   a. Go back and review the abilities, skills, and interests self-assessments and see if there is a pattern in line with your motivational gift.

   b. Have a heightened awareness of things you do well and that come easily for you.

   c. Begin to develop your strengths through mentorship, formal study or training, and/or home study, including tapes and books.

9. Recognize your weaknesses and place them here in your journal. These are the areas you will want to temper as you mature.

   a. Determine your weaknesses in social interaction and learn to temper or develop in those areas.

Mark 9:23
*All things are possible to him
who believes.*

---

    b. Recognize the areas in which you are not naturally gifted and determine how to delegate and defer to others for help.
10. Begin to identify job and work situations in which your motivational gift can be fully expressed.
    a. You may already be in the best situation to express your motivational gift.
    b. You may need to see your present job from a different perspective.
    c. It may mean slightly adjusting your present job responsibilities and duties.
    d. You may need to believe God to be reassigned to a new position in the company or to find a new job. If this is the case, be patient and allow God to direct your steps.
11. Begin to allow your gift to be expressed in your service to other people.
    a. Serve God and the body of Christ in areas that are supported by your motivational gift.
    b. Serve your family, friends, and community, and perform civic duties using your motivational gift.

Section C

If you do not possess the motivational gift of Giver, consider the following.

12. Identify those in your circle of family and friends who possess this motivational gift.

_____   _____

_____   _____

Colossians 3:23
And whatever you do,
do it heartily, as to the Lord, and not to men.

_____

_____   _____

_____   _____

13. Study the differences in patterns and behavior between the Giver and yourself.
    a. The ability to understand others and effectively interact with people is a fundamental key to success.
    b. Think about times you could have misunderstood a Giver because you did not understand the gift.
    c. Purpose to attempt to understand the Giver rather than judging them.
    d. Learn to accept and not reject the perspective of the Giver even though it is different from your own.
    e. Pray and ask God to give you wisdom on how to properly interact with the Giver motivational gift.
14. Study the strong characteristics of the Giver motivational gift and build these characteristics into your behavior patterns.
    a. Learn the positive behaviors of the Giver.
    b. Avoid the negative behaviors of the Giver.
15. Determine ways to utilize or rely on a Giver to help you accomplish your goals and tasks.
    a. Determine the ways someone of this motivational gift can help compensate for your weaknesses.
    b. Determine if you should completely delegate a task to the Giver or just ask for advice or help.
    c. Learn to embrace each motivational gift for the unique wisdom and perspective toward life that God gave them.

_____

Jeremiah 29:11
For I know the thoughts that I think toward you, says the LORD;
thoughts of peace and not of evil, to give you a future and a hope.

_____

DAY 7: JOURNAL

_____

_____

_____

_____

_____

_____

_____

_____

_____

_____

_____

_____

_____

_____

Psalm 35:27 (NLT)
But give great joy to those who have stood with me in my defense.
Let them continually say, "Great is the LORD, who enjoys helping his servant."

Job 36:11
*If they obey and serve Him, They shall spend their days
in prosperity, And their years in pleasures.*

Psalm 37:23
The steps of a good man are ordered by the LORD,
And He delights in his way.

Jeremiah 33:3
Call to Me, and I will answer you,
and show you great and mighty things, which you do not know.

_____

_____

_____

_____

_____

_____

_____

_____

_____

_____

_____

_____

_____

_____

Philippians 4:13
*I can do all things through Christ
who strengthens me.*

_____

_____

_____

_____

_____

_____

_____

_____

_____

_____

_____

_____

_____

_____

_____

Matthew 21:22
And whatever things you ask in prayer,
believing, you will receive.

_____

DAY SEVEN : PAGE 108

WORKPLACE
WISDOM

PURPOSE

DAY EIGHT

In Day 8, the motivational gifts of Administrator and Compassion are outlined. God has called the Administrator to facilitate, administrate, and organize, while the Compassion gift is anointed by God to attend to and care for the emotional needs of others. Day 8 also answers the questions and challenges often faced in attempting to narrow down your motivational gift.

8

God's Unique Motivational Gifts – Administrator / Compassion

ADMINISTRATOR

- God created the Administrator to facilitate, organize, and administrate.

- Administrators tend to be more project oriented than people oriented.

- Administrators are highly skilled at visualizing how people and systems work together to accomplish a goal.

- Administrators understand, respect, and honor authority.

COMPASSION

- God created the Compassion motivational gift to attend to and care for the emotional needs of others.

- The Compassion motivational gift is very people oriented and tends to be highly perceptive and sensitive to the emotional needs of others.

- The Compassion motivational gift feels drawn to people in need and enjoys doing thoughtful things for others.

 See Day Eight: God's Unique Motivational Gifts — Administrator/Compassion in *How to Discover Your Purpose in 10 Days.*

PRAYERFUL REFLECTION FOR THE
ADMINISTRATOR MOTIVATIONAL GIFT

Lord, I thank You for creating me in Your own image with an ability to oversee and manage multiple projects; and I thank You for anointing me to delegate and lead.

Father, I accept this gift. I realize that the gifting You have placed inside of me is vital in carrying out Your plans and purposes on earth. Therefore, I thank You for gifting me with a natural ability to develop and manage projects and people, make excellent decisions, and communicate well.

I count it an honor and a privilege that You have empowered me to be visionary with an ability to work well alone and with others.

Now that I know how I am wired, I commit myself to developing and maturing in my gift. From this day forward, I will seek

Proverbs 16:3 (NLT)
Commit your work to the LORD, and then
your plans will succeed.

jobs, volunteer activities, and hobbies that will further enable me to mature in my gifting.

I realize that there are strengths and weaknesses inherent in each of the motivational gifts. Therefore, I will strive to maximize my strengths and temper my weaknesses by working to cultivate the positive attributes of the other motivational gifts into my life.

I value other people's perspectives, and as I continue learning about their motivational gifts, I will embrace them, for I know each of us has a unique responsibility from You. In Jesus' name, I pray. Amen.

PRAYERFUL REFLECTION FOR THE COMPASSION MOTIVATIONAL GIFT

Lord, I thank You for creating me in Your own image with an innate ability to sense the emotional needs of others; and I thank You for anointing me to express myself in artistic and creative ways.

Father, I accept this gift. I realize that the gifting You have placed inside of me is vital in carrying out Your plans and purposes on earth. Therefore, I thank You for gifting me with a natural ability to care for others, do thoughtful things for others, and maintain peaceful and harmonious surroundings.

I count it an honor and a privilege that You have empowered me with a sensitive and considerate attitude.

Now that I know how I am wired, I commit myself to developing and maturing in my gift. From this day forward, I will seek jobs, volunteer activities, and hobbies that will further enable me to mature in my gifting.

I realize that there are strengths and weaknesses inherent in each

---

Psalm 16:11

You will show me the path of life; In Your presence is fullness of joy; At Your right hand are pleasures forevermore.

---

of the motivational gifts. Therefore, I will strive to maximize my strengths and temper my weaknesses by working to cultivate the positive attributes of the other motivational gifts into my life.

I value other people's perspectives, and as I continue learning about their motivational gifts, I will embrace them, for I know each of us has a unique responsibility from You. In Jesus' name, I pray. Amen.

DAY 8: ADMINISTRATOR ACTION PLAN

Please use the *Self-Assessment Workbook* as needed to complete the following items in your action plan.

Section A
1. Perform the Administrator self-assessment.
2. Attempt to determine if you are an Administrator motivational gift.
    a. If yes, continue to section B, question 3 and complete the steps. (Skip section C.)
    b. If no, continue to section C, question 12 and complete the steps.
    c. If unsure, continue to complete all sections concerning the remaining motivational gifts (see Days 5-8) and complete all motivational gift self-assessments.

Section B
3. If you have successfully determined that you are an Administrator, congratulations! You have been wired by God to facilitate, organize, and administrate. That is a blessing!

Ephesians 2:10 (NLT)
For we are God's masterpiece. He has created us anew in Christ Jesus, so that we can do the good things He planned for us long ago.

The identification of your motivational gift is very helpful in determining your God-given purpose.

4. Pray and thank God for how He made you; for you have been fearfully and wonderfully made. God needed you to be this way to fulfill His plans and purposes for your life.

5. Decide to accept yourself as God made you. Many people don't accept the way God made them. They desire to become another motivational gift rather than who God made them to be. That will slow up your process of development.

6. Review the characteristics of the Administrator motivational gift and begin to observe your motivational gift in operation in your life. Write your observations here in your journal.
   a. Observe why and how you make decisions.
   b. Observe how you respond to situations.
   c. Observe your thought processes.
   d. Observe your natural interactions with people.
   e. If your behaviors don't line up with the general characteristics, re-evaluate yourself to determine if you need to re-identify your motivational gift.
      Remember: You do not have to perfectly match every characteristic in order to be that motivational gift.

7. Have those closest to you (spouse, parents, children, close friend) confirm your motivational gift.
   a. Have those close to you review the characteristics of the Administrator and confirm whether you line up with them.
   b. Those close to you will have an independent opinion of how you really act.

Proverbs 16:9 (AMP)
A man's mind plans his way, but the Lord directs his steps and makes them sure.

---

    c. If you don't line up, start over in the identification process.

8. After confirming your gift, determine your strengths and begin to develop them at a higher level. List them here in your journal.

    a. Go back and review the abilities, skills, and interests self-assessments and see if there is a pattern in line with your motivational gift.

    b. Have a heightened awareness of things you do well and that come easily for you.

    c. Begin to develop your strengths through mentorship, formal study or training, and/or home study, including tapes and books.

9. Recognize your weaknesses and place them here in your journal. These are the areas you will want to temper as you mature.

    a. Determine your weaknesses in social interaction and learn to temper or develop in those areas.

    b. Recognize the areas in which you are not naturally gifted and determine how to delegate and defer to others for help.

10. Begin to identify job and work situations in which your motivational gift can be fully expressed.

    a. You may already be in the best situation to express your motivational gift.

    b. You may need to see your present job from a different perspective.

    c. It may mean slightly adjusting your present job responsibilities and duties.

Jeremiah 1:5
Before I formed you in the womb, I knew you; Before you were born,
I sanctified you; I ordained you a prophet to the nations.

---

     d. You may need to believe God to be reassigned to a new position in the company or to find a new job. If this is the case, be patient and allow God to direct your steps.

11. Begin to allow your gift to be expressed in your service to other people.

     a. Serve God and the body of Christ in areas that are supported by your motivational gift.

     b. Serve your family, friends, and community, and perform civic duties using your motivational gift.

Section C

If you do not possess the motivational gift of Administrator, consider the following.

12. Identify those in your circle of family and friends who possess this motivational gift.

_____   _____

_____   _____

_____   _____

_____   _____

13. Study the differences in patterns and behavior between the Administrator and yourself.

     a. The ability to understand others and effectively interact with people is a fundamental key to success.

Proverbs 4:7

*Wisdom is the principal thing; Therefore get wisdom.
And in all your getting, get understanding.*

---

    b. Think about times you could have misunderstood an Administrator because you did not understand the gift.

    c. Purpose to attempt to understand the Administrator rather than judging them.

    d. Learn to accept and not reject the perspective of the Administrator even though it is different from your own.

    e. Pray and ask God to give you wisdom on how to properly interact with the Administrator motivational gift.

14. Study the strong characteristics of the Administrator motivational gift and build these characteristics into your behavior patterns.

    a. Learn the positive behaviors of the Administrator.

    b. Avoid the negative behaviors of the Administrator.

15. Determine ways to utilize or rely on an Administrator to help you accomplish your goals and tasks.

    a. Determine the ways someone of this motivational gift can help compensate for your weaknesses.

    b. Determine if you should completely delegate a task to the Administrator or just ask for advice or help.

    c. Learn to embrace each motivational gift for the unique wisdom and perspective toward life that God gave them.

DAY 8: COMPASSION ACTION PLAN

Please use the *Self-Assessment Workbook* as needed to complete the following items in your action plan.

Psalm 139:14
I will praise You, for I am fearfully and wonderfully made,
Marvelous are Your works, and that my soul knows very well.

Section A

1. Perform the Compassion self-assessment.
2. Attempt to determine if you are a Compassion motivational gift.
   a. If yes, continue to section B, question 3 and complete the steps. (Skip section C.)
   b. If no, continue to section C, question 12 and complete the steps.
   c. If unsure, continue to complete all sections concerning the remaining motivational gifts (see Days 5-8) and complete all motivational gift self-assessments.

Section B

3. If you have successfully determined that you are a Compassion motivational gift, congratulations! You have been wired by God to attend to and care for the emotional needs of others. That is a blessing! The identification of your motivational gift is very helpful in determining your God-given purpose.
4. Pray and thank God for how He made you; for you have been fearfully and wonderfully made. God needed you to be this way to fulfill His plans and purposes for your life.
5. Decide to accept yourself as God made you. Many people don't accept the way God made them. They desire to become another motivational gift rather than who God made them to be. That will slow up your process of development.
6. Review the characteristics of the Compassion motivational gift and begin to observe your motivational gift in operation in your life. Write your observations here in your journal.
   a. Observe why and how you make decisions.

Mark 9:23
*All things are possible to him
who believes.*

---

b. Observe how you respond to situations.

c. Observe your thought processes.

d. Observe your natural interactions with people.

e. If your behaviors don't line up with the general characteristics, re-evaluate yourself to determine if you need to re-identify your motivational gift.

   Remember: You do not have to perfectly match every characteristic in order to be that motivational gift.

7. Have those closest to you (spouse, parents, children, close friend) confirm your motivational gift.

   a. Have those close to you review the characteristics of the Compassion and confirm whether you line up with them.

   b. Those close to you will have an independent opinion of how you really act.

   c. If you don't line up, start over in the identification process.

8. After confirming your gift, determine your strengths and begin to develop them at a higher level. List them here in your journal.

   a. Go back and review the abilities, skills, and interests self-assessments and see if there is a pattern in line with your motivational gift.

   b. Have a heightened awareness of things you do well and that come easily for you.

   c. Begin to develop your strengths through mentorship, formal study or training, and/or home study, including tapes and books.

9. Recognize your weaknesses and place them here in your journal. These are the areas you will want to temper as you mature.

Colossians 3:23
And whatever you do,
do it heartily, as to the Lord, and not to men.

---

    a. Determine your weaknesses in social interaction and learn to temper or develop in those areas.

    b. Recognize the areas in which you are not naturally gifted and determine how to delegate and defer to others for help.

10. Begin to identify job and work situations in which your motivational gift can be fully expressed.

    a. You may already be in the best situation to express your motivational gift.

    b. You may need to see your present job from a different perspective.

    c. It may mean slightly adjusting your present job responsibilities and duties.

    d. You may need to believe God to be reassigned to a new position in the company or to find a new job. If this is the case, be patient and allow God to direct your steps.

11. Begin to allow your gift to be expressed in your service to other people.

    a. Serve God and the body of Christ in areas that are supported by your motivational gift.

    b. Serve your family, friends, and community, and perform civic duties using your motivational gift.

Section C

If you do not possess the motivational gift of Compassion, consider the following.

12. Identify those in your circle of family and friends who possess this motivational gift.

Jeremiah 29:11

For I know the thoughts that I think toward you, says the LORD; thoughts of peace and not of evil, to give you a future and a hope.

_____   _____

_____   _____

_____   _____

_____   _____

13. Study the differences in patterns and behavior between the Compassion and yourself.
    a. The ability to understand others and effectively interact with people is a fundamental key to success.
    b. Think about times you could have misunderstood a Compassion because you did not understand the gift.
    c. Purpose to attempt to understand the Compassion rather than judging them.
    d. Learn to accept and not reject the perspective of the Compassion even though it is different from your own.
    e. Pray and ask God to give you wisdom on how to properly interact with the Compassion motivational gift.
14. Study the strong characteristics of the Compassion motivational gift and build these characteristics into your behavior patterns.
    a. Learn the positive behaviors of the Compassion.
    b. Avoid the negative behaviors of the Compassion.
15. Determine ways to utilize or rely on a Compassion to help you accomplish your goals and tasks.
    a. Determine the ways someone of this motivational gift can help compensate for your weaknesses.

_____

Psalm 35:27 (NLT)
But give great joy to those who have stood with me in my defense.
Let them continually say, "Great is the LORD, who enjoys helping his servant."

_____

b. Determine if you should completely delegate a task to the Compassion or just ask for advice or help.

c. Learn to embrace each motivational gift for the unique wisdom and perspective toward life that God gave them.

DAY 8: JOURNAL

_____

_____

_____

_____

_____

_____

_____

_____

_____

_____

_____

Job 36:11
If they obey and serve Him, They shall spend their days in prosperity, And their years in pleasures.

Psalm 37:23
The steps of a good man are ordered by the LORD,
And He delights in his way.

_____

_____

_____

_____

_____

_____

_____

_____

_____

_____

_____

_____

_____

_____

_____

Jeremiah 33:3
Call to Me, and I will answer you,
and show you great and mighty things, which you do not know.

_____

DAY EIGHT : PAGE 125

_____

_____

_____

_____

_____

_____

_____

_____

_____

_____

_____

_____

_____

Philippians 4:13
*I can do all things through Christ
who strengthens me.*

DAY EIGHT : PAGE 126

_____

_____

_____

_____

_____

_____

_____

_____

_____

_____

_____

_____

_____

_____

_____

Matthew 21:22
And whatever things you ask in prayer,
believing, you will receive.

_____

_____

_____

_____

_____

_____

_____

_____

_____

_____

_____

_____

_____

_____

_____

_____

_____

Proverbs 16:3 (NLT)
Commit your work to the LORD, and then
your plans will succeed.

_____

DAY EIGHT : PAGE 128

WORKPLACE
WISDOM

DAY EIGHT : PAGE 129

PURPOSE

DAY NINE

By Day 9, you should have begun to discover your God-given purpose. With this exciting revelation, you will learn how important it is to become more developed and mature in your purpose. It is God's desire that you dominate to His glory in your vocation. To do this, you must mature in your life work. Not only will you please God, you will also live a satisfied and fulfilled life.

9

*Maturing in Your Purpose – The Adult Years

- The greater your God-given purpose, the more preparation or time you may need in order to fulfill it.

- The adult years are pivotal in a person's life. It is during these years that God expects you to walk in the fullness of your purpose and become excellent in it.

- Maturing in your purpose requires diligence, time, patience, and prayer. The most successful and highly developed individuals recognize this and take the necessary steps to ensure their optimal success.

- To become successful and highly developed, you must:
  - Select excellent mentors
  - Participate in focused volunteer activities
  - Develop the strengths and temper the weaknesses of your motivational gift
  - Obtain advanced job training
  - Pursue continuing education opportunities
  - Work with seasoned professionals and consultants who are leaders in your vocation

 See Day Nine: Maturing in Your Purpose — The Adult Years in *How to Discover Your Purpose in 10 Days.*

PRAYERFUL REFLECTION
Lord, I thank You that You have called me to do a great and mighty work on earth and I thank You that I am equipped to do this work with specific God-given talents, gifts, and abilities. I know that Your gifts and calling are without repentance, and I understand that this means no matter what my age, the awesome things You have placed on the inside of me are still there, and waiting to be put into action.

I pray that as I operate in my life work, You will be with me and anoint and prosper the work of my hands, just as you did for Joseph. I also ask for wisdom in selecting mentors who will work to keep me focused on my life purpose. Guide me in choosing volunteer activities that will engage my gifts, talents, and abilities to Your glory.

Lord, I pray that I will get a revelation of how to become a

Psalm 16:11
You will show me the path of life; In Your presence is fullness of joy; At Your right hand are pleasures forevermore.

developed individual and sit down in my seat of purpose to be all that You have called me to be.

I purpose to be a blessing to others behind me. As Abraham was blessed to be a blessing, so shall I be a blessing to many because of Your favor upon my life, my preparation and excellent fulfillment of my assignment.

Father, I know that You are counting on me to be my best, so I pray that You will cause information to be made readily available to me. Show me what I need to do, and I will apply Your Word to any obstacles that may arise so that I may be a person after Your own heart. In Jesus' name, I pray. Amen.

DAY 9: ACTION PLAN

Please use the *Self-Assessment Workbook* as needed to complete the following items in your action plan.

1. Pray and ask the Lord to reveal the areas that you need to mature and become more highly specialized in. Write them here in your journal.
2. Identify and engage highly developed mentors in your vocational area.
3. Find compatible volunteer activities that will support the growth of your natural talents, gifts, and abilities.
4. Find specific ways to increase your vocational knowledge. Place them here in your journal for reference. You may:
   a. Take continuing education courses
   b. Read trade journals

Ephesians 2:10 (NLT)
*For we are God's masterpiece. He has created us anew in Christ Jesus,
so that we can do the good things He planned for us long ago.*

---

    c. Read books

    d. Pursue on-the-job training

5. Identify and make a list here in your journal of all the hobbies you may become actively involved in that will result in the maturation and development of your abilities and talents.

6. As you mature in your purpose, become a mentor to someone else to help them in their process of development.

7. Get involved in activities that will keep you abreast of technological and industry changes and advances. Involvement may include trade associations or unions. Charities may also provide the opportunity for industry growth.

DAY 9: JOURNAL

Proverbs 16:9 (AMP)
A man's mind plans his way, but the Lord directs
his steps and makes them sure.

_____

_____

_____

_____

_____

_____

_____

_____

_____

_____

_____

_____

_____

_____

Jeremiah 1:5
Before I formed you in the womb, I knew you; Before you were born,
I sanctified you; I ordained you a prophet to the nations.

_____

_____

_____

_____

_____

_____

_____

_____

_____

_____

_____

_____

_____

Proverbs 4:7
Wisdom is the principal thing; Therefore get wisdom.
And in all your getting, get understanding.

_____

DAY NINE : PAGE 136

Psalm 139:14
I will praise You, for I am fearfully and wonderfully made,
Marvelous are Your works, and that my soul knows very well.

DAY NINE : PAGE 137

_____

_____

_____

_____

_____

_____

_____

_____

_____

_____

_____

_____

_____

Mark 9:23
*All things are possible to him
who believes.*

_____

DAY NINE : PAGE 138

_____

_____

_____

_____

_____

_____

_____

_____

_____

_____

_____

_____

_____

_____

_____

Colossians 3:23
And whatever you do,
do it heartily, as to the Lord, and not to men.

_____

_____

_____

_____

_____

_____

_____

_____

_____

_____

_____

_____

_____

_____

_____

Jeremiah 29:11
*For I know the thoughts that I think toward you, says the LORD;
thoughts of peace and not of evil, to give you a future and a hope.*

DAY NINE : PAGE 140

WORKPLACE
WISDOM

PURPOSE

DAY TEN

There is a great life work that the Lord is counting on you to fulfill. There is also an awesome destiny that God has prepared before the foundation of the world for you to realize. So, this power-packed series concludes on Day 10 centering on how to make your purpose a reality in your life.

10

Fulfilling the Greatness Within

- You were fearfully and wonderfully made in the very image and likeness of God Himself.

- God has placed inner greatness within you that yearns for expression. It is reflected in your motivational gift, your ruling passion, and your natural gifts and abilities.

- God created you to fulfill a great and mighty purpose on earth — you were formed with an awesome destiny.

- It is only when you operate in your purpose that your life has true significance and meaning.

- Work is a gift from God and He expects you to dedicate yourself to the life work that He has called you to fulfill.

- You are called to spend time adding to the lives of others through your life service/ministry. You minister to others through your relationship with God and your family, your church, your workplace, your civic duty, and community service.

- Your life message evolves and changes as you grow and mature in your life work. It is the conscious or subconscious statement of the very essence of your being. You have a God-ordained purpose, but your life message is what you choose to live.

 See Day Ten: Fulfilling the Greatness Within in *How to Discover Your Purpose in 10 Days.*

PRAYERFUL REFLECTION

Dear Heavenly Father, I thank You and give You praise and glory that before the foundation of the world, You knew who I would be. Thank You Lord for loving me so very much that I would be created with a purpose, fully equipped with everything I need to fulfill Your purpose on the inside of me. I thank You gracious Father, that you would bring parents, mentors, early jobs, hobbies, opportunities, and exposure into my life to allow me to blossom and manifest the greatness that You placed inside of me.

Thank you Lord for the blood of Jesus that protects me and keeps me from hurt, harm, and danger. Thank You Lord for the blood that

Psalm 35:27 (NLT)
But give great joy to those who have stood with me in my defense.
Let them continually say, "Great is the LORD, who enjoys helping his servant."

cleanses me and washes off every obstacle that tries to come against the work that You have planned for me to perform.

I thank You Lord God that You have given me a motivational gift and that You have uniquely equipped me to grow and develop in the gifts that You have placed inside of me. Thank You that You have called me to greatness because You are great and I am made in Your likeness and image. For this, I give You praise and glory.

I am ever grateful to You God for giving me a great destiny. I purpose to walk this destiny out and live a legacy that is glorifying and pleasing to You, that I may be a blessing to others. I will never take for granted that You have given me a purpose and I commit to walk my purpose out. I love You Lord and will bless Your holy name forever. In Jesus' name and by His blood, I pray. Amen.

DAY 10: ACTION PLAN

Please use the *Self-Assessment Workbook* as needed to complete the following items in your action plan.

1. Pray and thank God for creating you with a specific purpose.
2. Write out your life purpose here in your journal.
3. Here in your journal, state your present life message. Also, state what you want your life message to be in the future.
4. Create and write a vision statement here in your journal of what God has placed on your heart to accomplish in your lifetime.
5. Prayerfully reflect on how you currently spend your time. Prayerfully reflect on what adjustments need to be made to

Job 36:11
If they obey and serve Him, They shall spend their days in prosperity, And their years in pleasures.

ensure that your time is being spent most effectively to the glory of God.

6. Seek the Lord's direction on how to move along the continuum of life purpose so that you will get into the stage of Life Purpose Fulfilled.

7. Identify ways you can become highly developed in your purpose and list them here in your journal.

8. Spend time in prayer and ask the Lord to reveal to you the areas you need to focus on to mature and develop in your purpose. Write them here in your journal. Work hard to be faithful.

9. Make a decision to be excellent in all of your areas of life service, including your:
    a. Relationship with God
    b. Witness
    c. Prayers for others
    d. Family
    e. Church
    f. Workplace
    g. Friends
    h. Community
    i. Civic duty

IF YOU DO NOT KNOW THE LORD, GIVE YOUR HEART TO JESUS TODAY

The Word of God says in Romans 10:9-10, that "if you shall confess with your mouth the Lord Jesus, and believe in your heart that God has raised Him from the dead, you will be saved. For with the heart

---

Psalm 37:23
The steps of a good man are ordered by the LORD,
And He delights in his way.

---

one believes unto righteousness, and with the mouth confession is made unto salvation."

If you do not know the Lord as your Savior, you can recite this simple prayer of salvation: I believe Jesus Christ is the Son of God, that He carried my sins for me, and that He died on the cross at Calvary. He was put in a grave, but I believe He is risen and alive right now. Lord Jesus, come into my heart and save me now. I believe in my heart, therefore I confess with my mouth that Jesus Christ is now my personal Lord and Savior. Thank you Lord for saving me now. In Jesus' name, I pray. Amen.

(If you prayed this prayer, congratulations! We are so very excited for you. We want to e-mail you a free e-book to help you on your Christian journey. Please contact us at info@eaganbooks.com.)

DAY 10: JOURNAL

_____

_____

_____

_____

_____

_____

_____

Jeremiah 33:3
Call to Me, and I will answer you,
and show you great and mighty things, which you do not know.

Philippians 4:13
I can do all things through Christ
who strengthens me.

Matthew 21:22
And whatever things you ask in prayer,
believing, you will receive.

_____

_____

_____

_____

_____

_____

_____

_____

_____

_____

_____

_____

_____

_____

_____

Proverbs 16:3 (NLT)
Commit your work to the LORD, and then
your plans will succeed.

———————

DAY TEN : PAGE 150

Psalm 16:11
You will show me the path of life; In Your presence is fullness of joy;
At Your right hand are pleasures forevermore.

Ephesians 2:10 (NLT)
For we are God's masterpiece. He has created us anew in Christ Jesus,
so that we can do the good things He planned for us long ago.

DAY TEN : PAGE 152

_____

_____

_____

_____

_____

_____

_____

_____

_____

_____

_____

_____

_____

_____

Proverbs 16:9 (AMP)
*A man's mind plans his way, but the Lord directs
his steps and makes them sure.*

_____

_____

_____

_____

_____

_____

_____

_____

_____

_____

_____

_____

_____

_____

_____

_____

Jeremiah 1:5
Before I formed you in the womb, I knew you; Before you were born,
I sanctified you; I ordained you a prophet to the nations.

_____

DAY TEN : PAGE 154

WORKPLACE
WISDOM

DAY TEN : PAGE 155

Share Your Personal Testimony with Us

We would love to hear about the awesome things that the Lord has done in your life as a result of your reading and applying the principles we have shared in this book. Let us know how this book has affected you and what other information you would like us to share in future material at info@eaganbooks.com.

We also invite you to send us your e-mail address, so that we may send you a complimentary copy of The Eagan Report on a periodic basis. For more information, visit our web site: www.eaganbooks.com.

God bless you!

Remember, God is expecting greatness in your life!

Other Books Authored by the Eagans Include:

Dominating Business
How to Prosper on Your Job

Anointed for Work
Using the Tools from Sunday to Succeed on Monday

How to Determine Your Motivational Gift
Learn How God Wired You

Dominating Money
Personal Financial Intelligence

The Character of Success
26 Characteristics of Highly Successful People

The Word @ Work, Volumes I & II
Scriptures for the Workplace

How to Discover Your Purpose in 10 Days
God's Path to a Full and Satisfied Life

How to Discover Your Purpose in 10 Days
Self-Assessment Workbook

Upcoming Books Include:

Godly Leadership in the Workplace

The Road to the Wealthy Place
Dominating Money in Business

Terminating Conflict
God's Solutions to Resolving Conflict Permanently

All titles are available on-line at www.eaganbooks.com.
Also available: CDs and DVDs.
For more information, E-mail us at info@eaganbooks.com
or call 1-877-EAGANS1 (324-2671).